Highlights
Hidden Pictures

PET PUZZLES
DELUXE

See pages
78–88
for crafts,
recipes, and
activities!

T0016756

HIGHLIGHTS PRESS
Honesdale, Pennsylvania

Knock, knock.
Who's there?
Eileen.
Eileen who?
Eileen over to pet the dog.

Knock, knock.
Who's there?
Cat.
Cat who?
Cat you just let me in?

ruler

boot

mitten

pie

envelope

These pets love to get outside. Can you find the objects hidden in this city scene?

Knock, knock.
Who's there?
Dogs go.
Dogs go who?
No, dogs go woof!

Knock, knock.
Who's there?
Isabelle.
Isabelle who?
Isabelle on the cat's collar?

Art by Jeffrey Crowther

crayon

fish

crown

broccoli

3

Busy Bunnies

See if you can find all the hidden objects before the workers are done for the day.

toothbrush

cherry

sock

candle

teacup

flag

crown

lollipop

baseball cap

comb

crayon

ruler

golf club

crescent moon

nail

wishbone

Art by Mike DeSantis

No Bones About It

These dogs are digging for treats. Can you help them find 14 bones hidden in the backyard?

Take Two

Where are you when you fall asleep reading a book?

Under the covers

What are two things you can't have for breakfast?

Lunch and dinner

Each of these scenes contains 12 hidden objects, which are listed below. Find each object in one of the scenes, then cross it off the list.

banana	die	light bulb	seashell
bell	doughnut	lollipop	slize of pizza
button	fan	nail	slice of watermelon
cane	heart	octopus	sock
carrot	horseshoe	paper clip	spring
comb	ladder	sailboat	wishbone

Art by Paula Bossio

Feline Friend

It's fun having a cat to keep you company!
Find the objects hidden in this bedroom.

ice-cream cone

candle

comb

candy cane

wedge of orange

doughnut

vase

crown

Art by Tamara Petrosino

Poodle Puzzler

Fifi just moved into this fantastic 12-room doghouse. How can Fifi get from the front door to the back door by going through each room only once?

Pet Palace

zipper

cracker

hourglass

ruler

mushroom

piece of candy

cookie

game piece

piano

closed umbrella

arrow

crown

drinking straw

dustpan

wedge of lemon

ant

piece of watermelon

nail

Art by Christine Schneider

11

$ PEANUT $
BUTTER

Crab Condos

golf club

fried egg

ax

shovel

fishhook

mitten

needle

slice of pizza

boomerang

adhesive bandage

pencil

envelope

These crab families are trying to find new shell homes.
See if you can find all the hidden objects before the new family moves in!

saxophone

hockey stick

pennant

banana

artist's brush

mug

crescent moon

thimble

test tube

heart

beehive

wedge of lemon

Art by Daryl Collins

Sneaky Slitherer

Sam Snake must have been very hungry! Try and find the objects hidden in this messy kitchen.

flag

crescent moon

flashlight

drinking straw

baseball cap

ladder

heart

nail

skateboard

gravy boat

rolling pin

mitten

sailboat

party hat

comb

wedge of lemon

horseshoe

sock

Art by Kyle Beckett

Tic Tac Row

What do you think the cats in each row (horizontally, vertically, and diagonally) have in common?

How do you spell "mousetrap" with only three letters?

C-A-T

What do invisible cats drink?

Evaporated milk

Each of these small scenes contains **6** hidden objects from the list below. Some objects are hidden in more than one scene. Can you find the **6** hidden objects in each scene?

Hidden Object List

The numbers tell you how many times each object is hidden.

adhesive bandage (5)

carrot (2)

comb (4)

crescent moon (4)

envelope (4)

feather (2)

hockey stick (3)

piece of popcorn (4)

pitcher (2)

screw (2)

slice of pizza (2)

waffle (2)

BONUS
Two scenes contain the exact same set of hidden objects. Can you find that matching pair?

Art by Brian Michael Weaver

pennant

fork

ice-cream cone

piece of popcorn

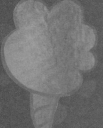

cotton candy

nail

acorn

Poppy Prancing

Can you find all the hidden objects before it's time to return to the barn?

Art by Julissa Mora

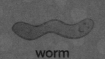

heart

whistle

spoon

spool of thread

worm

bagel

cupcake

Dance with Me

Can you find at least 10 differences between these two pictures?

Pets at the Fair

Which things in this picture are silly? It's up to you!

Art by Kelly Kennedy

What pets are playing in this scene? Draw what you think here.

Art by Dave Clegg

New Shoes

Can you find at least 20 differences between these two pictures?

What do baby bunnies learn in school?

The alfalfa-bet

Why was the bunny upset?

He was having a bad hare day.

24

What is a cat's favorite treat?

Mice cream

What does a cat use to stir pancake batter?

A whisk-er

Art by Katie McDee

Hot Diggity Dogs

sailboat

paper airplane

stamp

taco

hanger

flashlight

wedge of cheese

ring

comb

artist's brush

ruler

flyswatter

These hot dogs love eating hot dogs!
Can you find all of the hidden objects before the cats crash the party?

kite

pencil

book

lollipop

rake

belt

sock

mug

envelope

wristwatch

cupcake

Art by Kelly Kennedy

boot

glove

crescent
moon

spatula

bell

knitted hat

A Ribbety Band

These frogs are rocking out. Can you find all the hidden objects before their show is over?

mallet

sailboat

teacup

scissors

seashell

heart

butter
knife

slice of
pie

flowerpot

sock

crown

28

Art by Gary Mohrman

Can you find the dog? Can you also find 12 tiny mice?

Art by Travis Foster

Doggie Vacation

fishhook

baseball cap

fish

piece of popcorn

shoe

bowl

heart

These dogs are having a great time at the beach!
Look for the objects hidden in their vacation photo.

crescent
moon

book

kite

necktie

crown

needle

spoon

Art by Catherine Copeland·Photo by damedeeso/iStock

clock

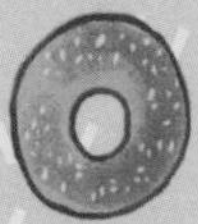

bagel

basketball

slice of lemon

Pet Rescue

Good thing there are so many superheroes around! See if you can find all the hidden objects.

Art by Deborah Melmon

ball of yarn

bowling ball

button

target

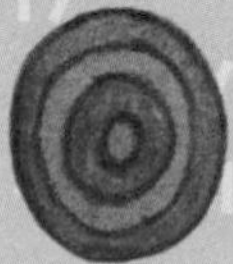

Leaping Lizard

This little lizard got on the roof! Help it crawl down the building and find its way back inside to its friends.

Art by Mattia Cerato

Downward Dog

oar

candy corn

banana

plate

golf club

peanut

stamp

snow cone

ring

needle

horseshoe

horn

golf tee

spoon

cupcake

wedge of
cheese

drinking
straw

candle

fishhook

Art by Laura Ferraro Close

cinnamon bun

key

sailboat

button

crescent moon

snowman

game piece

Art by Katie McDee

37

Dogs or Cats?

flashlight

mushroom

magic wand

bowling ball

oar

rope

bowling pin

musical note

jug

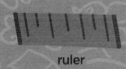

ruler

HOT DOG

Art by James Loram

baguette

muffin

Reading Buddies

These animals like to read too!
See if you can find all the hidden objects.

fish

crescent moon

pencil

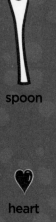
sailboat

spoon

heart

crescent moon

needle

candle

banana

toothbrush

Art by Tamara Petrosino

40

Tic Tac Row

What do you think the dogs in each row (horizontally, vertically, and diagonally) have in common?

Art by Jennifer Morris

Which bones do dogs not like?

Trombones

What dog loves to take bubble baths?

A shampoodle

Take Two

Where do cats and dogs go on vacation?

Pets-ylvania

What wears a coat in the winter and pants in the summer?

A dog

42

Each of these scenes contains 12 hidden objects, which are listed below. Find each object in one of the scenes, then cross it off the list.

bacon	drinking straw	ladder	pencil
belt	envelope	light bulb	sailboat
bowling Ball	fish	lightening bolt	snail
carrot	golf club	magnifying glass	toothbrush
crescent Moon	grapes	mitten	wedge of orange
crown	ice-cream bar	mug	worm

Cat Gymnastics

These feline gymnasts are training hard for their meet. Look for all the hidden objects.

candle

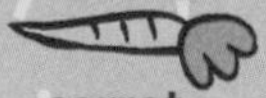

carrot

flag

closed umbrella

hockey stick

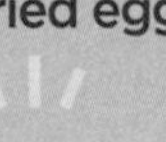

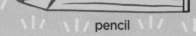

fried egg

fork

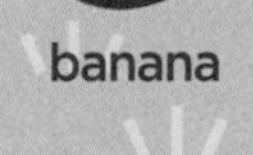

banana

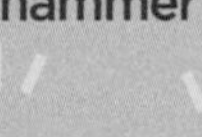

hammer

pencil

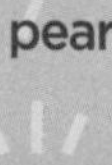

pear

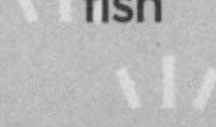

fish

crown

Dapper Dogs

Cat Corner Cafe
Which things in this picture are silly?
It's up to you!

Art by Josh Cleland

Skating Scout

Scout is taking his skateboard for a spin.
Who is skateboarding with him? Draw them here.

Art by Dave Clegg

Feeding Farm Friends

Who do horses like to visit?

Their neigh-bors

What is a horse's favorite salad dressing?

Ranch

Why do cowboys ride horses?

They're too heavy to carry.

Why don't people build robot horses?

They go haywire.

Art by Julissa Mora

Adopt a Friend

candle

mitten

safety pin

domino

horseshoe

comb

number seven

potato

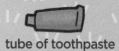
tube of toothpaste

fishhook

elbow noodle

slice of pie

mushroom

vase

Art by Dana Regan

waffle

muffin

feather

envelope

banana

51

Can We Keep Them?

Surprise—Barkley Bunny has some new fluffy babies! Find all the hidden objects.

envelope

pencil

ruler

yo-yo

ax

fishhook

seashell

feather

sailboat

broom

magnet

nail

test tube

slice of pizza

artist's brush

magician's wand

paper clip

Art by Daryll Collins

52

Frog Frenzy

Can you find the turtle? Can you also find 12 flies?

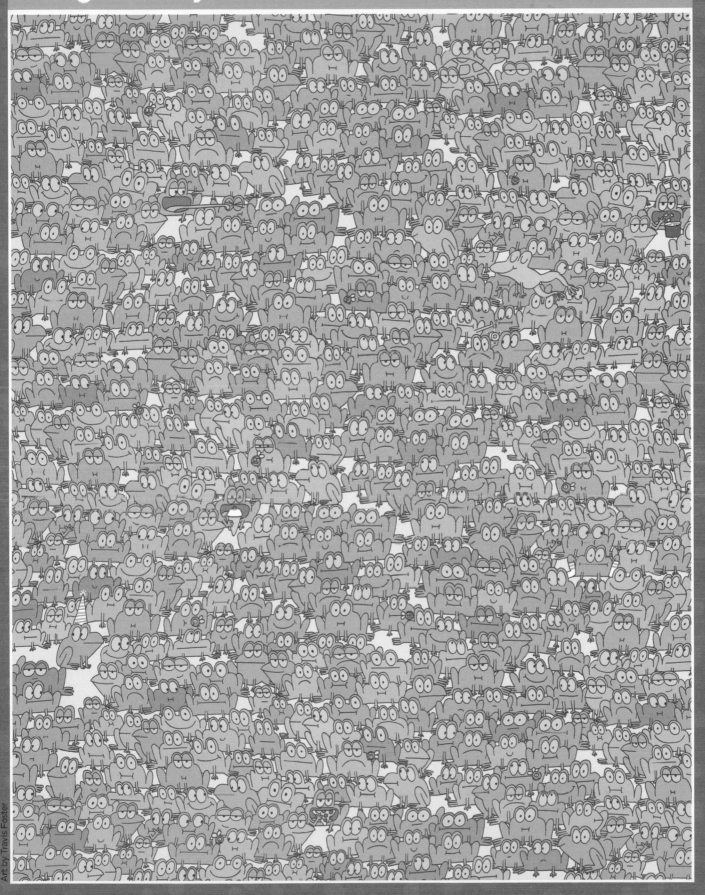

Art by Travis Foster

Hidden Object List

The numbers tell you how many times each object is hidden.

baseball (2)

cane (4)

crescent moon (4)

fish (3)

fried egg (2)

heart (4)

mitten (2)

mug (3)

ruler (3)

slice of bread (3)

tack (2)

wedge of cheese (3)

BONUS
Two scenes contain the exact same set of hidden objects. Can you find that matching pair?

Art by Jannie Ho

55

Pooch Party

Happy Birthday, Max! Can you find the hidden objects before Max blows out the candles?

fish

slice of pizza

pencil

pencil

Art by Jef Czekaj

banana

ring

skateboard

kite

Hamster House

Freckles is hungry. Can you help him find his route to the table? (He can pass by papers and seeds.)

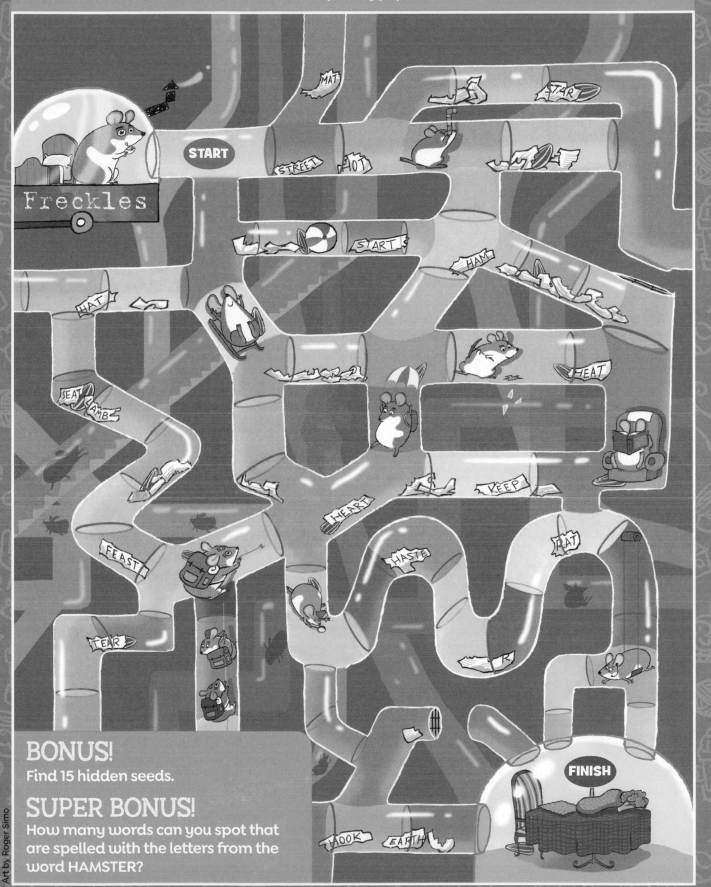

BONUS!
Find 15 hidden seeds.

SUPER BONUS!
How many words can you spot that are spelled with the letters from the word HAMSTER?

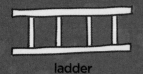
ladder

envelope

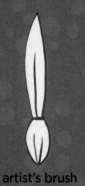
artist's brush

basketball

wishbone

scarf

Creature Chorale

mug

domino

muffin

piece of popcorn

glove

crown

So that's what pets do when people aren't home!
See if you can find all the hidden objects before their concert ends.

slice of pie

hockey stick

toothbrush

crescent
moon

belt

slice of
pizza

spoon

slice of lemon

pencil

light bulb

ruler

horseshoe

Silly Pet Shop

Farm Pets

Knock, knock.
Who's there?
Neigh.
Neigh who?
Neigh-body
listens to me!

Knock, knock.
Who's there?
Farmer.
Farmer who?
Farmer people
here than
last week.

toothbrush

butter knife

pitcher

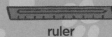
ruler

Knock, knock.
Who's there?
Chesterfield.
Chesterfield who?
Chesterfield full of sheep.

Knock, knock.
Who's there?
Moo.
Moo who?
Which are you?
A cow or an owl?

Art by Tim Budgen

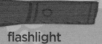

flashlight

sock

slice of pie

bowling pin

Lizard Volleyball

Bump, set, spike! Can you find all the hidden objects?

domino

hockey stick

handbag

test tube

drinking straw

bell

flag

ruler

fishhook

artist's brush

glove

slice of pie

wishbone

boomerang

crescent moon

heart

feather

flowerpot

Art by Gary Mohrman

Tic Tac Row

What do you think the horses in each row (horizontally, vertically, and diagonally) have in common?

Art by Carolina Farias

How could a cowboy ride in on Friday, stay three days, then ride out on Friday?

Friday was the name of his horse.

What has four legs and flies?

A horse in the summertime

Art by Catherine Copeland • Bulldog Photo by damedeeso/getty, Sock Photo by issaurinko/getty

Going for a Ride

Noah loves riding with his pet horse Annie.
See if you can find all the hidden objects.

cinnamon bun

snowman

sock

paper clip

Art by Patrick Girouard

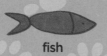
fish

mitten

comb

lime

Pet Picasso

Can you find at least 10 differences between these two pictures?

Neighborhood Pets

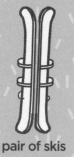
match

pair of skis

lighthouse

basketball

raindrop

computer mouse

pacifier

camera

fried egg

boat

paint roller

rabbit

70

necktie

flag

ice-cream cone

zucchini

plunger

ear of corn

Art by Iryna Bodnaruk

teddy bear

winter hat

puzzle cube

comb

handbag

dinosaur

71

Different Dogs

Can you find at least 14 differences between these two pictures?

What dogs don't bark?

Hot dogs

What dog can tell time?

A watch dog

What is a dog's favorite kind of pepper?

Howlapeño

What is a dog's least favorite place to go?

A flea market

Fish Food

leaf

slice of pizza

apple

ruler

glove

magnet

teacup

domino

wedge of orange

grapes

heart

mushroom

Time to feed the fish!
Can you find all the objects hidden below before the fish eat all their food?

spoon

bowl

horseshoe

candle

snow cone

lime

slice of pie

ladder

hat

banana

baseball cap

crown

Art by Brian White

Time for a Checkup

See if you can find all the hidden objects during the vet's visit.

vacuum cleaner

vest

volcano

snake

violin

vine

vase

volleyball

greeting card

broccoli

Art by Mattia Cerato

There are 15 mice hidden in this scene. Can you find them all?

Art by Travis Foster

Puzzling PETS

You Need
★ Ruler
★ Craft foam
★ Paper
★ (Optional) Wiggle eye or button

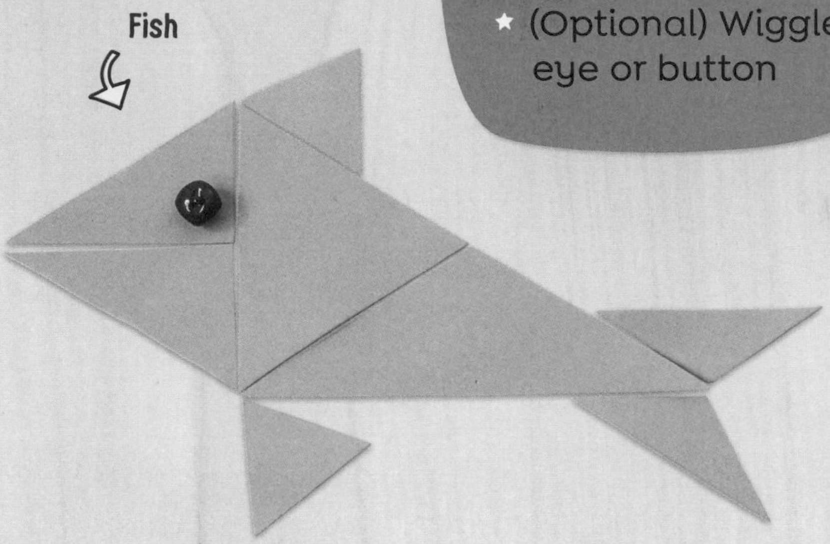

Fish

1 Using a ruler as a straight-edge, draw the lines shown below on a sheet of craft foam.

2 Cut out the triangles.

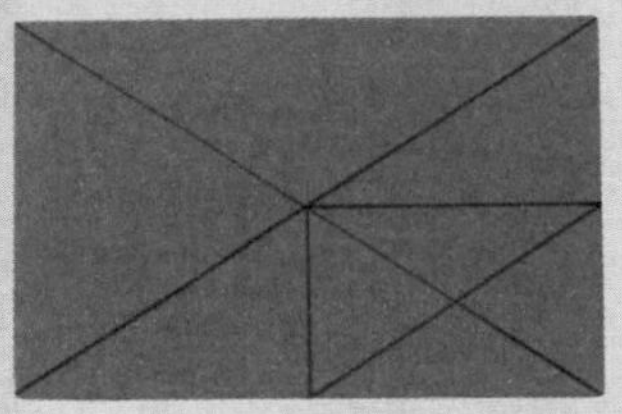

Aardvark

Cat

Add a wiggle eye or a button.

To Play

On paper, arrange the triangles to create a shape. Trace its outline. Give the outline and triangles to a friend. Challenge them to create the same shape. Take turns challenging each other.

Ask an adult for help with anything sharp.

"Feed the Frog" Game

You Need
★ A large round container
★ Green and black paper
★ Glue
★ Poster board
★ Plastic spoon

1. Glue green paper around a large round container.

2. Draw a frog with a large mouth on poster board. Cut out the frog, and decorate. Glue the frog to the container.

3. To make "flies," crinkle small pieces of black paper.

To Play   Play with a friend. Use a plastic spoon to flick the fly! Whoever gets a fly into the frog's mouth in the fewest flicks wins.

Ask an adult for help with anything sharp.

Tabletop Horseshoe Game

You Need

* ★ Corrugated cardboard
* ★ Posterboard
* ★ Cardboard tube
* ★ Duct tape
* ★ Glue
* ★ Colored paper

1 For the game's base, cut two 9-inch-by-13-inch rectangles from corrugated cardboard. Cover one rectangle with poster board. Cut a 1-inch hole in its center.

2 For the post, cut one side of a short cardboard tube lengthwise. Roll the tube tight so it fits into the 1-inch hole. Cover the tube with duct tape, leaving the bottom inch ucovered.

3 Cut four slits in the untaped part of the tube. Stick the slits through the hole. Fan them out and tape them to the underside of the covered cardboard rectangle.

4 Glue the second cardboard rectangle under the first (to cover the tape).

5 For each player, cut two horseshoes from corrugated cardboard. Cover each set with colored paper. Use a different color for each player.

To Play

Players take turns tossing their horseshoes at the post. Once all the horseshoes have been tossed, tally up the points. Horseshoes that encircle the post are three points. Horseshoes that land on the game's base but don't encircle the post are one point. The player with the highest score wins.

Ask an adult for help with anything sharp.

PARROT PUPPETS

You Need
* Paper
* Pins
* Fleece fabric
* Fabric glue
* Felt

1. To make a template, place one hand on paper with your thumb out and fingers together. Trace it, leaving an extra 1/2 inch of space the whole way around. Cut out the template.

2. Use pins to attach the mitten template to two layers of fleece fabric. The pins should go through both layers of fleece. Cut around the template through the layers.

3. Remove the pins and template. Glue the edges of the fleece shapes together with fabric glue, leaving the cuff open. Let mitten dry.

4. Repeat steps two and three to make the second mitten. Turn the mittens inside out.

5. Cut feathers, beaks, and eyes out of felt. Glue parrot decorations to the mittens.

6. Have fun making these parrot puppets talk!

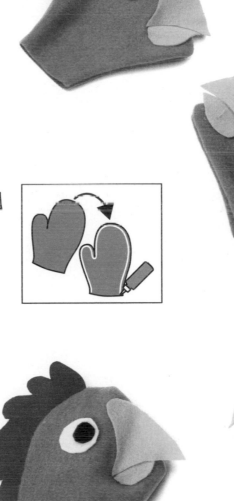

Ask an adult for help with anything sharp.

Special Snacks for Pet Pals

Make the paw-fect treat for your animal buddy.

Check with your vet before feeding new foods to your pet.

Cat Snack

Mix together 2 tablespoons of tuna, 1 tablespoon of shredded cheese, and 1 teaspoon of oatmeal. Press the mixture into a muffin-tin cup. Carefully tap the treat out and place it on a cat dish. Top with small cat treats.

Pup Cake

Mix together 2 tablespoons of dry dog food, 1 tablespoon of peanut butter, and 1 tablespoon of mashed banana. Press the mixture into a muffin-tin cup. Carefully tap the treat out and place it on a dog dish. Add banana slices. Top with a dog treat.

Towering Treat

For other animals, slice up their favorite fruits and vegetables. Stack the pieces in layers. Top with their favorite treat.

Purr-ty Pudding
rice pudding
banana
blueberry
strawberry
raspberry
kiwi
raisin

Lion in the Lunch
cottage cheese
banana
pineapple
grape
raisin
kiwi
red pear
cantaloupe

Pet FACES Snack
(for people!)

Hummus Hound
hummus
cucumber
black olive
grape tomato
sweet pepper

You Need
★ Hummus, rice pudding, or cheese
★ Fruits and vegetables

1 Flatten a scoop of cottage cheese, hummus, or rice pudding on your plate, or start with a slice of cheese.

2 For features or details, select foods that will taste good with the base. Try fruits with cottage cheese or rice pudding, and vegetables with hummus or cheese.

3 Cut the toppings into decorative shapes. Use the shapes to make pet faces. Then chomp!

Ask an adult for help with anything sharp.

bunny MAGIC game

A Game for 2 Players

You Need

- Round oatmeal container
- Black and white paper
- Red craft foam
- Glue
- Cardboard tube
- Pompoms
- Wiggle eyes
- Paper plate
- Black poster board
- White paint pen or colored pencil
- Metal fastener

 For the hat, cut off and discard the top half of an round oatmeal container. Glue black paper to the sides and bottom. Tape on a paper brim. Add a band of red craft foam below the brim.

 For the rabbit game pieces, cut two sections from a cardboard tube. Decorate them with white paper, pompoms, and wiggle eyes. Draw on facial features.

Ask an adult for help with anything sharp.

To Play

Give each player a wand and a rabbit game piece. During each turn, both players spin. Players add the two numbers that their arrows landed on. The player with the higher sum moves his or her rabbit forward one space. The first player whose rabbit hops into the hat wins.

 For the wands, cut two long rectangles from black poster board. Divide them into nine spaces using the white paint pen or colored pencil. Glue a white square to the top space. Write "Start" in the bottom space.

 For the spinner, divide a paper plate into eight sections. Number them 1–8. Cut a double-pointed arrow from poster board, punch a hole in the center, and use a metal fastener to attach it to the plate. Decorate the spinner with paper and pompoms.

Choco-Cherry Mice

1 Add 1 cup of chocolate chips and 2 tablespoons of coconut oil to a microwave-safe bowl. Microwave for 30 seconds. Remove bowl with oven mitts, and stir. Continue microwaving in 30 second bursts until chocolate is completely melted.

2 Hold the cherry stem and dip cherry into melted chocolate. Place on wafer cookie as shown.

3 Stick the pumpkin seed ears and chocolate kiss to the melted chocolate, as shown. Use a toothpick to dip into the melted chocolate and draw eyes onto the chocolate kiss.

4 Keep mice refrigerated in a covered container before serving.

You Need
* ★ Chocolate chips
* ★ Coconut oil
* ★ Maraschino cherries
* ★ Pumpkin seeds
* ★ Chocolate kisses
* ★ Wafer cookies
* ★ Oven mitts
* ★ Toothpick

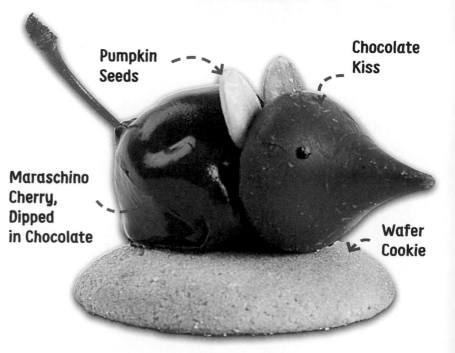

Pumpkin Seeds

Chocolate Kiss

Maraschino Cherry, Dipped in Chocolate

Wafer Cookie

Pencil Box PUP

You Need
* Long cardboard tube
* Thin cardboard
* Glue
* Paint
* Craft foam
* Wiggle eyes
* Air-dry clay

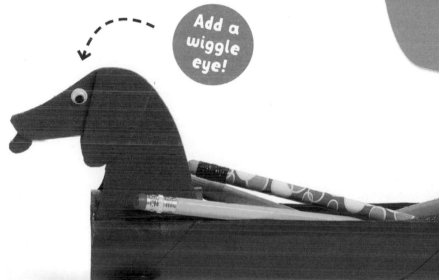

Add a wiggle eye!

 Cut a rectangular opening in a long cardboard tube.

 Trace around the ends of the tube onto thin cardboard. Cut out the circles. Glue one to each end of the tube.

 Paint the tube. Cut a head, tongue, and tail from craft foam. Glue them on. Add wiggle eyes.

 Mold four round legs from air-dry clay. Glue them on.

You Need
* Squirt bottles
* Foam sheets
* Adhesive glue dots
* Wiggle eyes

Fish Friend Spritzers

1 For each fish spritzer, cut two identical fish shapes from foam sheets. Decorate them with foam shapes. Add foam teeth and wiggle eyes.

2 Use adhesive glue dots to stick the fish shapes on opposite sides of a squirt bottle. Make sure the fish's mouth lines up with the nozzle. Fill with water, then spritz yourself to stay cool.

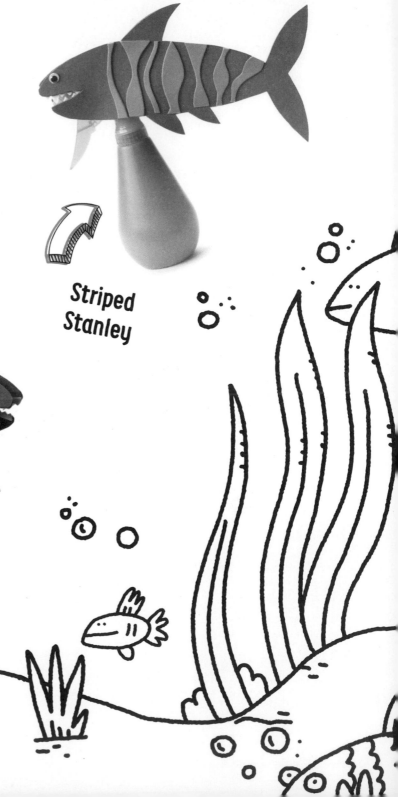

Striped Stanley

Fantastic Finn

Ask an adult for help with anything sharp.

▼ Pages 2–3

▼ Page 4

▼ Page 5

▼ Pages 6–7

▼ Page 8

▼ Page 9

Answers

▼ Pages 10–11

▼ Pages 14–15

▼ Page 16

▼ Page 17

Sleeping
Has a bowl
Green Collar

Sleeping
Has a Toy

Sleeping
Has a Bed
Solid Color

Stretching
Has a Bowl

Stretching
Has a Toy
Green Collar
Solid Color

Stretching
Has a Bed

Has Kittens
Has a Bowl
Solid Color

Has Kittens
Has a Toy

Has Kittens
Has a Bed
Green Collar

▼ Pages 18–19

▼ Page 20

▼ Page 21

▼ Pages 24–25

▼ Pages 26–27

▼ Page 28

▼ Page 29

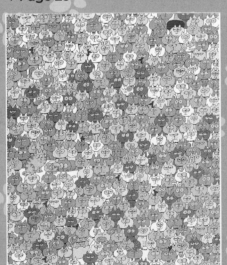

▼ Pages 30–31

Answers

▼ Page 32

▼ Page 33

▼ Pages 34-35

▼ Pages 38-39

▼ Page 40

Answers

▼ Page 41

▼ Pages 42–43

▼ Page 44

▼ Page 45

▼ Pages 48–49

▼ Pages 50–51

▼ Page 52

Answers

▼ Page 53

▼ Pages 54–55

▼ Page 56

▼ Page 57

▼ Pages 58–59

Answers

▼ Pages 62–63

▼ Page 64

▼ Page 65

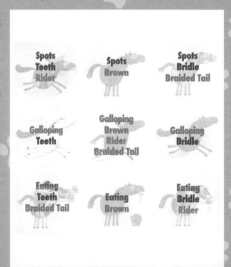

Spots Teeth Rider   Spots Brown   Spots Bridle Braided Tail

Galloping Teeth   Galloping Brown Rider Braided Tail   Galloping Bridle

Eating Teeth Braided Tail   Eating Brown   Eating Bridle Rider

▼ Pages 66–67

▼ Page 68

▼ Page 69

▼ Pages 70-71

▼ Pages 72-73

▼ Pages 74-75

▼ Page 76

▼ Page 77

Published by Highlights Press
815 Church Street
Honesdale, Pennsylvania 18431
ISBN: 978-1-64472-915-1
Manufactured in Shenzhen, Guangdong, China
Mfg. 05/2023
First edition
Visit our website at Highlights.com.
10 9 8 7 6 5 4 3 2
Cover art by Susan Batori
Craft photos by Guy Cali Associates, Inc., except animals (page 82) iStock/Getty Images Plus/adogslifephoto, party hats (page 82) iStock/Getty Images Plus/Nastco, banner, confetti, balloon (page 82) iStock/Getty Images Plus/leminuit

Frame Tips: Color the frames and cut them out. Tape a picture of your pet, dream pet, or favorite animal inside the frame windows. To hang a frame, tape a piece of string across the top, leaving slack to hang from a hook or a nail. To make a stand for a frame, cut a triangle from cardstock. Fold one side of the triangle to create a tab. Tape or glue the tab to the back of the frame. Ask an adult for help with anything sharp.

Stand Examples:

Make one tall stand. **OR** Make two smaller stands for extra support.

Tape or glue

Fold

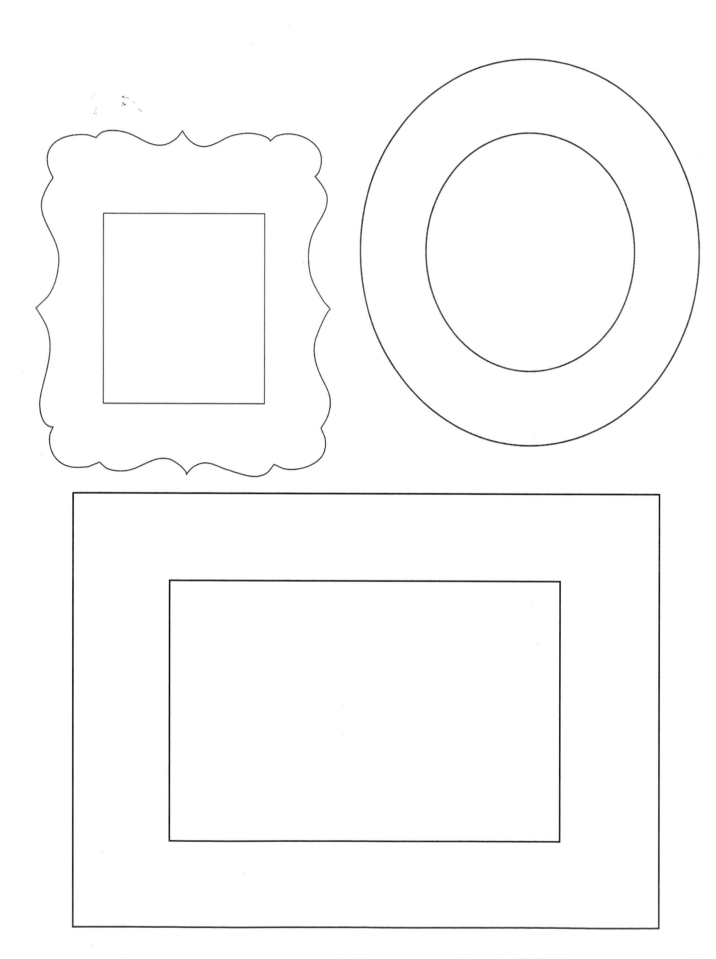

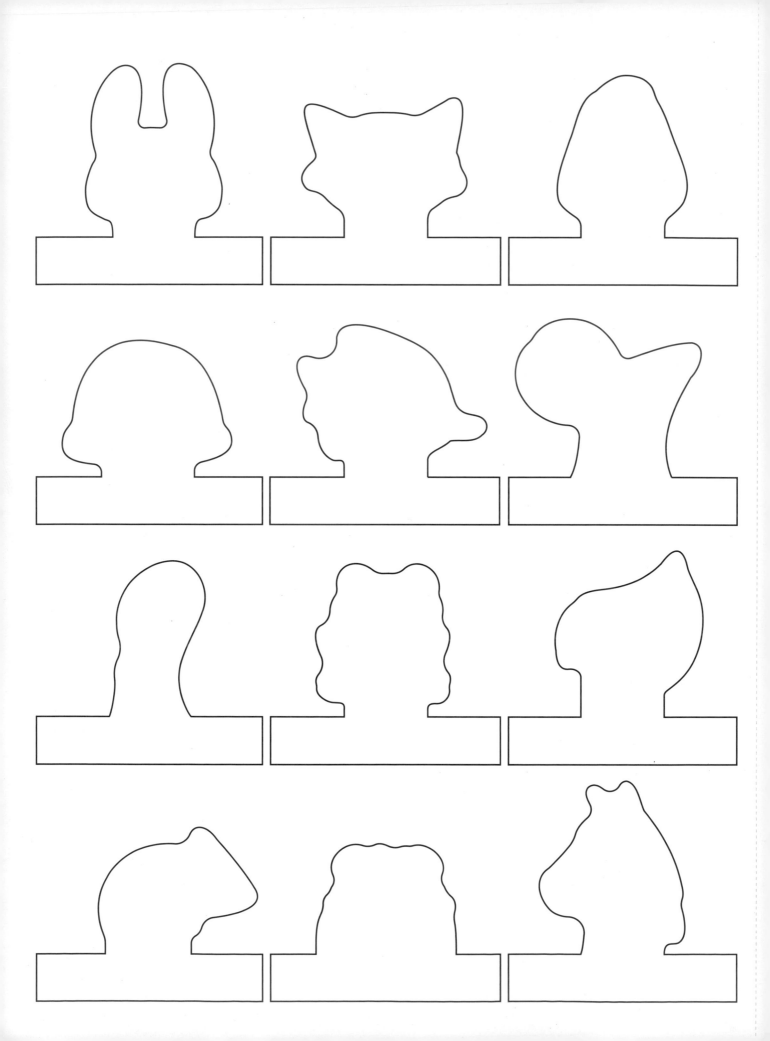

WOOF!

NEIGH!

meow

glub glub

TWEET

I LOVE MY PET!

SQUEAK

Highlights

WOOF!

meow

Best PET!

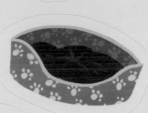

FURRY FRIEND

NEIGH!

TWEET

glub glub

SQUEAK